# Growing Your Family Tree

*"Sorting the Wheat from The Chaff"*

Brian W. Hurlburt

Copyright © 2019 Brian W. Hurlburt

# Table Of Contents



*"Sorting the Wheat from The Chaff"*

# DEDICATION
## Dedicated To Lucy Glover Mullen

There are a lot of people to whom this Book could be dedicated,
many of You know who You are and
I'll always be very thankful for all of You.

There is one, however, who may never know that
This Book is Dedicated to Her
My dear friend Lucy Glover Mullen.

Lucy and I spent many hours on the phone and in person
pouring over information related to our respective Families.

Families who intermingled long before either of us were ever thought of.
Families without whom we would never exist.

Families and Ancestors who have led to us being who we are At least by DNA,
and I often think in other respects too!

"Lucy believed that Everyone Counted"
Lucy had no "Unknowns" In Her Tree!

Many of Us include "Unknown" as the Family Name
When We don't know their Surname.
More often than not, these Unknown Surnames
belonged to Wives of our Male Ancestors.

Lucy believed Everyone Counted,
That Everyone was Important, and
That is why Lucy did not use "Unknown"
For unknown Surnames.
In Her Family Tree, Everyone was
"A Somebody"

Lucy made Me, and Everyone She met, feel like a Somebody!

*Lucille "Lucy" Elizabeth (Glover) Mullen 2 Feb 1954 - 28 Aug 2015*

# Foreward

After a rewarding career and retiring twenty years ago, I began to formulate a
"Retirement Plan" that had to include keeping an active, open mind
and doing something for others.

I had seen the following meaningful verse:
GREAT people talk about IDEAS
AVERAGE people talk about THINGS
SMALL people talk about OTHER PEOPLE,
and then sadly, there are people
who love to talk about themselves.

I decided to keep My mind active by leaving a legacy for
My children and grandchildren,
so began growing My Family Tree and also my Husband's,
in order to find and preserve the family "Roots".

I began with the following philosophy in mind:
Before you assume, Learn the facts
Before you judge, Understand why
Before you hurt someone, Feel
Before you speak, Think.

Growing a Family Tree, involves all of the above.

Searching for facts was more difficult twenty years ago
and a resource book would have been most welcome.

My search led me to meeting Brian, first on-line, then telephone and finally in person.
Our "meant to be" meeting has given us many years of working together.
I was able to recognize his talent for helping others, his well developed marketing skills
and his keen learning and organizational skills.

I had seen a quote by Ben Carlson:
"Happiness doesn't result from what we GET, but from what we GIVE."
Knowing that Brian had much to give to help others search for their "Roots",
I encouraged Him to write this book for the benefit of others.

Brian has sorted the wheat from the chaff in this most informative book on "Growing
Your Family Tree".
Beginning and Seasoned genealogists alike, will find it an essential, informative read!
Many thanks, Brian. May You gain "Happiness" from what You have given Us!

*By Dianne Perrin B.Ed.*

# Proem

I was blessed with having Senior Parents, a natural curiosity, and desire to learn.
I began doing Family History Research and Genealogy in 1991.
Having Senior Parents was a Blessing, and know that
it gave me many opportunities I would not otherwise have had.

This Book has been written, after much prompting by many people, over the years.
I started my Family History and Genealogy Work in 1991, over 27 years ago!

Had anyone told me then that I'd still be working on this today,
or that I'd come to write a Resource, or "How To" Book,
I would have probably laughed and told them they were crazy.

After all at that point the longest I'd ever done anything was probably the twelve years I
spent in Grade School. That, as a result of Parents who were either really interested in
my getting a good Education, or who, as my Friend, and Cousin's Wife, Dianne once
said, "I think They would have sent You to School."

Dianne has come into my life perhaps not to replace Lucy, but to help fill the Void.

Dianne, being honest and not afraid to speak her mind, once told me that She was
pretty sure, "They would have sent me to School."
She was, shall we say, half joking! (I Think)

What she meant was with my natural curiosity and hunger for knowledge,
They would have sent me to School simply to get some peace and quiet!
Perhaps that's why she is encouraging me so now!

Regardless of why Dianne is so encouraging, and remains such a great friend, is a bit of
a Mystery, but even after 7 years we remain friends, we work together on many
Genealogical Challenges and seem to have the ability to coerce each other into doing
the things that perhaps should have been done sooner, rather than later,
even when those things have been on the Bucket List for 27 Years!

So, while over the years, many have asked, I've written this Book at Dianne's request,
and given her the opportunity to write the Foreward.

Either way, I am Thankful for Dianne, and Her Husband Stan!

# A Journey of a Thousand Miles, begins with a Single Step!

This is about to become Your Legacy!
Something You can create in a relatively short period of time,
but take the rest of your lifetime perfecting! Perhaps many Lifetimes,
as Your Work may help benefit those who come after You.

Not only Immediate Family, but for Cousins and future Researchers following
in your footsteps. Many of whom You may never know,
but who may come to know You!

Much as it is now, for You, and what You're about to discover about Ancestry,
Your Ancestors, and the Roots of Your Family, and Your Family Tree!

When it comes to researching Your Family's History it's best to start with those
closest to You, and You do that with a Single Step!
Pick up the phone, send an email, or go visit, your oldest Family Members!
Seniors often welcome the company, and they are the most valuable source of
immediate information.Take it from me, don't put it off!

I've done that on many counts, and have always come to regret it!

Don't wait, grab a piece of paper, write down what You know.
Your Name, Your Parents Names, and if Possible Your Grand Parents Names.

If You don't know who your Grand Parents are, or were,
ask Your Parents, Uncle or Aunt, or Older Neighbour.

Now, while it's fine to start with a simple piece of paper, or notebook,
or even RecipeCards,

You'll soon want to find a Database for Your Work.

I recommend Legacy Family Tree.

# Legacy Family Tree Genealogy Software

By the way, when I started researching,
I used looseleaf and duotang. I used that for my rough notes,
and later added my info, a person at a time onto Recipe Cards.

Recording Name, Address, Phone, Marriage, and Spouse Name,
on each Card, and then I cataloged them.

Today, it's much easier to start with a Database,
like Legacy Family Tree.

It combines a great database experience,
with great customer service, and many features
that provide on going benefits.

It's the program I've been using for at least the past 20 Years!

Perhaps I should mention that
I started researching My Own Family back in 1991, some 28 Years Ago!

I've learned a lot, made many mistakes, found surprises, not all good,
and encountered many Brick Walls!

Brick Walls are what We call Dead Ends, when we are unable to find further
information! Many things may lead to Brick Walls, like when we were trying to
find my 3rd Great Grand Father, James Ward born about 1818 in England.

There were so many James Wards at the time, in England, it was difficult
to know which one was ours! Another reason for Brick Walls is Name Changes,
like when James Ward came to North America,
seemingly changing his Surname from Mills to Ward!

One other thing I should mention is,
if You decide to do this research You may find some Dark Surprises!
Don't let them discourage You! Just Record Them!

I record my findings using Legacy…

Legacy Family Tree Genealogy Software

I'm not going to rewrite the Book or Create a New Video about Legacy
because they do an incredible job of doing that themselves.
The Good People at Legacy have taken the time to create the tools You need.

Legacy provides far more than a Data Base!
• Hinting - Legacy 9 searches through billions of records from key websites -
FindMyPast, FamilySearch, GenealogyBank, and MyHeritage.
• Stories - Preserve the stories of your ancestors or your own.
The new Stories tool lets you record, organize and print
multiple stories for any of your ancestors.
• Hashtags - Create unlimited hashtags to describe your ancestors.
Then search for or print a report of everyone who shares that hashtag.
• FindAGrave.com Searching - One-click access
to your ancestor's Find A Grave memorial.
Create a list of people in your tree with or without Find A Grave IDs.
• And much, much more!

You can get Your
Free Legacy Family Tree Software
on our Website at

growingyourfamilytree.com

# Now What About Those Dark Surprises...

I'm tempted to say All Families have them!!
However, that is exactly the type of Assumption we never want to make!
We All Do It!

That said, there are a number of us who do have such things in our Ancestry,
whether it be direct line, or a Cadet Line. A cadet branch (or line) is a noble
House that descends from another noble House. They are usually created when
a younger member of a noble House, who is not the current heir of the family
seat, is granted lands and titles of his own.

For our purposes, and generally in Family History and Genealogy,
today a Cadet Line simply refers to a Cousin, or line of Cousins.
Yes, even our Cousins often have "That Person",
the so called "Black Sheep" of the Family.
Who may not be so "Royal".

It does, however, create some problems.

In dealing with sensitive situations like these, we may well encounter some
"Problems"'. However, these may not be the things that immediately come to
mind. The things I'm referring to are cover-ups by Family Members.

So, when we're talking to them we need to proceed with caution, treat such
situations delicately, and yet in most cases record at least the Person, if not the
situation.

Another area where "Dark Surprises" create problems is when researching
Historic Records. One would assume Historical Records would be exempt of
such things,but not necessarily so! Spellings, even Names, change over time!

Sometimes not as a cover-up, but often because Census Takers and Record
Keepers, and those they spoke to were limited in their spelling.
Names were often spelled as they were heard.

# Finding Available Records

Knowing what to look for, and where to look, is crucial to good research.
It is also very, very, important to take your time and record everything,
include your Sources, and don't skip ahead, or plan to come back later.

I've done this many times and have come to regret it!
Often costing myself a lot of time, and sometimes money, in the process.

I know how exciting it is, finding new information, family members,
making discoveries, and having ideas flood in as we learn where to go next!

Just be sure to take the time to make notes, to record your sources,
and You'll save yourself hours of work not having to go back later.
You've found the Source Document, or Person, or other Source,
now be sure to Record It.

Knowing what information is available is important.
If for no other reason You don't want to spend hours of your time
looking for information that is not currently available.

That leads me to another great reason for
always recording the Source when we first encounter it.
Whether our Source is a Person, Historic Record, or Other Source,
there is nothing saying it will be there, or even available when we return!

So, let's look what is usually available, and accessible for Public Access.
Typically, in most jurisdictions,
We need to get back at least 50 Years to find a Death Record,
75 Years for Marriage Records, and
100 Years for Birth Records.
There are exceptions to these Guidelines
and in some cases more recent Records are available to the Public.

However, some Records are only available to specific Family Members

So, we are often left to find information in Census Records.
Availability depends upon Jurisdiction.

The most recently available, Publicly available, Census Records
in Canada are those from 90 Years ago.

So in 2011 the 1921 Canadian Census Records were made available to the
Public.

More recent Census Records are available for the USA.
In 2010 the 1940 Census Records become available for public viewing.
This span being just 70 Years lends itself well to our Research.

* Here's a Tip that will help You
find the Descendants of those listed in the most recent Census Records,
especially those in the USA.

Let's say You are looking for information on my Birth Family…

I know my parents were Locke and Eleanor Hurlburt.
My Birth Mother was born circa 1930/31 in Halifax, Nova Scotia.
My Father was born in 1905, also in Nova Scotia.

Now, unfortunately I do not have access to My Mother's Birth Record,
and any Census She would have been in is not Publicly available.

However, my Father,
having been born in 1905
is recorded in the 1911 and 1921
Canadian Census Records.

Armed with that information
let's see what we can find out
about my Family by simply using Google.

# Google Can Yield Great Results

In fact if all we knew was that my parents were Locke and Eileen Hurlburt
we could still find information on their Family by using Google
and searching for "obit Locke and Eleanor Hurlburt".
Go ahead and do a Google now!


At the moment I see Results for My Mother, and two Brothers.


This gives me information I  need to find Family Members.


Finding these Family Member may lead me to Cousins,
especially older Cousins who may be able to lead me to more information.


Information that may not be available online or to the Public.


Even if I had only known my Father's Name from the Census Records,
I still could have "Searched" for "Obit Locke Hurlburt"
and it still would have led me to similar results
and extended Family Members.


These extended Family Members may lead me to information
Not otherwise available.


That is why it is often crucial to begin by talking to known Family Members,
Neighbours, and others, who may be able to help us find information on
Parents, Grand Parents, and sometimes even Great Grand Parents.


In fact when I started out Researching in Yarmouth County, Nova Scotia
it was at a time when the Elders in our Community remembered their Grand
Parents and mine, and a few remembered some of our Great Grand Parents.


This was crucial, as much of the previously researched information
ended at the Generation prior with just enough being remembered,
to match it up with the earlier research.

# Brown's A Sequel to Campbell's

In Yarmouth County, Nova Scotia, when I began researching there was an
earlier work, that of George S. Brown, namely
"Yarmouth, Nova Scotia: A Sequel to Campbell's History"
that was a valuable resource. While, as with any great work of it's kind,
there are possible errors in it, yet it still remains a valuable resource.
Providing much of the early history and Family information as well.

There are, likely, similar works available in your Area and a Visit to Your Local
Library, or Archives, is a great place to find such information.
Not only is it a good place to visit, the people are usually a wealth of
information, very helpful, helping You beyond the scope of this, or any Book.

I will always be very thankful to those who helped me at the
Izaak Walton Killam Memorial Library and the
Yarmouth County Museum and Archives

I'd love to mention Laura Bradley and Eric Ruff at the Museum and Archives,
and Blanche at the Library, but I know if I did that I'd miss others,
whom I'm also thankful for at both those locations.
So, I guess I'll forego mentioning anyone in specific.

Now that You've visited Your Relatives, and Elders in Your Community,
and spent time at your local Library, Museum, and Archives,
there is one place You may want to visit.

It is the Cemetery, where you should pay particular attention to,
and record, the Dates and Symbols on Family Grave Markers.
Paying attention to those buried nearby. They are often Relative!

You may have been surprised that I not only mentioned
Recording the Dates, but also the Symbols. Symbols, as well as Inscriptions,
may help indicate Religious, Fraternal, or other Group Affiliations.
These may lead you to nearby Churches, or other Organizations
who may have additional information that will aid you in your research.

# Churches, Community Groups, and Organizations

There are Churches, Community Groups, and Organizations that have kept
Records for Hundreds, if not Thousands of Years. Often these are
as reliable, perhaps even more reliable, than Government Records.

In my case, my Great Grand Father, Sidney D. Burrill, was a Free Mason,
and He held many Positions within the Brotherhood of Free and Accepted
Masons. In time I was able to acquire His Masonic Record, from a Cousin.

I have discovered that many organizations, including the
Freemasons, keep meticulous records and membership lists.
These are great resources when properly and respectfully approached.

Now that We've visited with the Family, the Elders, and the Dead,
we can begin looking at Online Resources and not only finding more
information, but also finding Sources to prove that information.

I'm used to promoting tools and resources that I earn a commission on,
for my Business, YourIndependentBusinessConsultant.com
but in this book most of the resources are free!

When I was starting my journey into Family History and Genealogy,
I had to find the best of the Free Resources to help me with my work.

So, don't feel You have to spend a lot of money. You don't!
There are a lot of Free Resources Online.

My Caution is be careful not to fall into a common trap of thinking
you're doing great things when you find and copy someone else's work!
I see it often!

Someone goes online to Ancestry, MyHeritage, or FamilySearch, sees  that
someone has done the work! So they copy it without checking the Source.
The same applies to other Websites too!

# Exercise Caution When Accessing Online Resources

There are lots of great Online Resources these days.
When I started back in 1991 there were few.


I spent many hours over many months going to
Libraries, Museum, Archives, Cemeteries, and
Talking with Family Members, Community Elders,
and other individuals who were also Researching.


I'm very thankful for all of these sources.
I'm also thankful that today
We can access much of this Information Online.


One Great, Free, Resource for online Research is
FamilySearch.org


When You go to their Site, concentrate on their Historical Records.
Start by Clicking the Search on their Site, then click on Records.


This will allow You to search actual Historical Records.
When using this feature try to keep in mind the Dates, and Time Frames
as previously mentioned for the records which are available to the Public.


Births prior to 100 years ago,
Marriages prior to 75 Years ago, and
Deaths occurring prior to 50 years ago.


Now, having said that,
FamilySearch is one place where it sometimes pays to search
even if the dates you have are more recent.


One example of this,
is the Search I just did for My Adopted Dad,
Victor Hurlburt Sr.

# FamilySearch.org

I just searched for Victor Hurlburt using his birth year of 1923
and found His birth, death, and place of burial linking to Find A Grave.


Victor Hurlburt Sr. & Enid Outhouse were my Mom & Dad,
My Adoptive Parents. The Headstone also shows my Adopted Mom's Dates.


Now, Google Search and get the Family Info!


**The Find A Grave Website**
provides a great, free, resource.
It was created by Jim Tipton in 1995
because he could not find an existing site that catered to
his hobby of visiting the graves of famous people.


At Find A Grave you'll find details about cemeteries and
individual memorials for many people buried in those cemeteries.
Memorials may include birth, death and burial information
as well as pictures, biographies, family information and more.


Membership is Free, and Members may contribute their knowledge
and leave remembrances completing the virtual cemetery experience.


I've also found some great Obituaries and related information there!


As with Family Search, Find A Grave also provides a Free Membership
and I encourage You to get a Membership at both of these places for Free!


When You have the Free Membership at FamilySearch
You can actually view the Original Historic Documents.


With Find A Grave Membership you can contribute,
and communicate with other Members,
and have a better overall experience with …

# Resources Well Worth Investigating

## Automated Genealogy
This is another Free Resource
for accessing Free Canadian Census Records.

The Census Records at Automated Genealogy include
Records for 1901, 1906, 1911, 1852 Canada, and 1851 Province of NB.

## The Library and Archives Canada
Provide Census Records from 1825 to 1921,
as well as a number of other Databases and other research tools.

I should also mention here that with all these Websites,
it often pays to look at the actual Document, not just the Transcriptions.

A Transcription is something that's been copied from the original Record.

We've already discussed how important it is to look at the original document,
and how even those Documents can have errors!

Add to that how easy it is to make mistakes
when transcribing information,
and we begin to see more clearly
why we should always see the original.

Other Records at Library and Archives Canada
Include:
Acts of Divorce, 1841-1968
Births, Marriages and Deaths Recorded in Canada
Marriage Bonds, 1779-1858 - Upper & Lower Canada

They even have Census Returns on Microfilm from 1770-1856

**Resources Well Worth Investigating**

# Giving Birth, Marriage, and Death Events A Place

Whether You start with the Census Records, or go directly to looking for
Events, and Vital Stats, like Birth, Marriage, and Death Records,
You'll want to work at comparing them.

When I was starting out researching I thought perhaps if I just skimmed the
census, or looked at most of them, I'd get the information I needed.
I was mistaken!

It is important to gather all the information, from all the Sources.

There are several reasons for this, among them are Name Spellings,
Residence Changes, Children who were born and died
or had other events happen between Census Years.

These things are easily missed when we try to skip a Census and other Records.
The area You are researching in, will determine
what resources are available in your local area.

Much of My Work, especially in the beginning, focused on
Nova Scotia, and Atlantic Canada,
as well as what We refer to as The New England States,
especially Massachusetts Pilgrim Ancestry.

I later discovered my Wampanoag Ancestry.

These kept me busy in my early days and
later my work spread to other areas.

Including most areas from Canada, the United States, and Mexico.
Even England, Ireland, Scotland, and Other Areas.

So, it is definitely Important to gather all available information.
For You never know where that missing link may lead You!

# Nova Scotia Vital Stats

Nova Scotia is where my Research began,
and perhaps the best place to find Vital Stats for Nova Scotia is at
Nova Scotia Historical Vital Statistics.

Nova Scotia began keeping Civil Registrations in 1763
with the introduction of procedures for obtaining a marriage license.
However, it was optional and the surviving records are incomplete.

In fact, I've found that prior to the 1800's
one is often best to concentrate on Church Records.

Church Records pertain to Christenings, Baptisms,
Marriages, Deaths and Burials.

However, there are a huge number of Records at
Nova Scotia Historical Vital Statistics from the mid 1800s on.
With the exception of 1877 to 1908, when
Nova Scotia allowed record-keeping to lapse for birth and death records.
Not all births, or deaths, or marriages, were recorded, regardless of Years.

Sometimes the Churches did a better job of keeping such information
and other times these Church Records were all lost,
through poor record keeping, theft, fire, or other reasons.

So, again, it is important not only to search out all available records,
but to compare all these records to build a better, more complete,
Picture of Your Family Tree.

We all have Brick Walls.
Some People seem to disappear, while others have no known Ancestry.
However, there are more Records being Digitized all the time and things have a
way of revealing themselves when we least expect it!

**Remain Hopeful!**

# Try Searching For Just Parts

When Searching Vital Stats, Census, and even Google,
Try searching for just parts
of the Words or Names, You're looking for.


When Searching for My 2nd Great Grand Parents,
Charles Dixon and Fanny Ward married c.1874
but I struggled to find their Marriage Record.


That's because when I was Searching for their full Names on
Nova Scotia Historical Vital Statistics
novascotiagenealogy.com


I couldn't find their Marriage Record while Searching their full names.


Even when I tried "Name Variations" like Frances for Fanny
I still couldn't find anything. till I learned to try Name Variations,
Different Spellings, and Parts of a Word, or Name.


**Searching Parts Becomes Very Important!**


When searching for Charles Dixon and Fanny Ward yielded No Results,
I discovered Searching Parts of a Word.
That's what led me to Success!


When I searched for just
C. Dixon
The Marriage Record showed up!


You'll find doing this will lead you to better search results,
even when Searching Sites like Google.


If You can't find the whole name, or word, then ...


**Try Searching for Just Parts.**

# Other Vital Sources...

Before we move on too much further,
I should tell You about a few more places to find vital Stats.
You'll, perhaps, want to search for similar sites and Sources in your Local Area.
As My Local Area is Atlantic Canada, I'm going to list some of those here…


### The Provincial Archives of New Brunswick
provides Vital Statistics from Government Records.


I truly like the NB Site as it allows You to Search,
and Freely Download the actual Documents!


Most places charge you for Documents, but
The Provincial Archives of New Brunswick
allows You to Download them for Free!
It's a Digital Copy,
but it sure is nice to be able to get
Records for Your Collection.


### The Prince Edward Island Public Archives
has an Online Database available for Searching.
You can use it for doing a Search,
but will have to purchase the actual Documents.


The Search Results do give transcribed basic information like
Name, Residence, and Marital Status, etc.


### Newfoundland Records
I prefer using the
"Newfoundland Vital Records, 1840-1949"
Which is one of many Collections available at …
FamilySearch.org

# A Few More Free Websites

I want to draw your attention to three more Free Websites.


These three Sites may become integral to Your Research,
especially if You're looking for Your Acadian Roots, or have already done a
DNA Test.
Further your research by looking into what other Researchers have already
done.
Those Three are :
1. WikiTree: The Free Family Tree
2. Généalogie Acadienne
3. Ged Match


At the time of writing, WikiTree is reported to include
19,751,211 profiles, and
5,089,738 with DNA test connections,
claiming to be edited by 599,728 genealogists
from around the world.


As with all Websites, be sure to use the Trees for leads,
but remember the information is only as reliable as the Sources cited.


### The Acadian Website, Généalogie Acadienne
Is an excellent Resource for anyone researching their Acadien Roots.


For those of us, who are not quite up on our French, a link at the top of Their
Page makes it is possible to View Acadian Genealogy in English


This is a Great Site, with a wealth of information.
at the time of this writing there are
783,513 individuals
314,055 families, and
22,651 surnames

# GedMatch

This brings us to a topic I'll delve into a little later,
but certainly no Book on Family History and Genealogy
would be complete today
without some discussion of DNA Testing.


GEDmatch provides DNA and genealogical analysis tools,
most of which are Free.
They do have some Premium Tools as well.


You'll need to upload your DNA Data or Genealogical (GEDCOM)
to make use of the tools there.


Registration is fairly simple,
and just requires your name, email and a password.


The Important thing here is that
in order to really benefit from DNA Matching Services
You will have to have previously had Your DNA Tested.


There are several places where You can get Your DNA Test done,
and while there are several types of DNA Tests …


The three most common types of DNA Tests are:
1. Y-DNA testing can be done by people with a Y chromosome
to research their "patrilineal" ancestry. This simply means that it can be done by
Men and Traces the Male Line of Ancestry.
Father, Grand Father, Great Grand Father, Etc., Etc.
2. mtDNA (Mitochondrial DNA) testing
traces a person's matrilineal (mother's female) ancestry.
However, unlike a Y-DNA test, everyone can take a mtDNA test.
3. Autosomal DNA Testing, the one done by Ancestry
analyzes most of your DNA and is more information-rich
than either Y-DNA or mtDNA tests.

# Time For A Test

The type of DNA Test you have done depends greatly on two things.
One is the type of information You're looking for, and the other is Your Sex.

The only Test that can not be done by Females is the Y-DNA Test.
It traces the Male Line and is described as only of benefit You're a Male.
Actually, that's not exactly right!

The Y-DNA Test can benefit Men and Women,
if it's a Man that takes the Test.

If You can identify a Brother, Father, or Grand Father,
who is willing to take a Y-DNA Test,
You may benefit from the Results.

Confirming Your "Male Line" may lead to other Male Cousins.
Cousins Whom You may then trace back to a Male Ancestor.

The further back the Common Ancestor is,
the more certain You can be, that Line is correct.

Now, if You are a Female, or a Male, and chances are you're one of those!
You may want to know more about Your Mother's Female Ancestry.
For this, You'll want to do a Mitochondrial DNA (mtDNA) Test.

The mtDNA Test basically does the same for tracing Your Female Line.
(Mother, Grand Mother, and Her Mother's Line)

For many years these two tests were all that was commonly available
and they often cost as much as a $1,000.00 or more!
However they have come down substantially in price.

There are places where You can get quality
Y-DNA and mtDNA Tests for about $200.00
Places like MyHeriage and FamilyTreeDNA

# Autosomal DNA Testing

I should probably point out...
that of the three types of DNA Testing,
I have only done the Autosomal DNA testing.

I may, at some point do my Y-DNA and mtDNA,
but for my purposes the Autosomal DNA Test provided by
Ancestry meets my needs.

I've been very pleased with my DNA Results and Cousin Matches.

My DNA Testing, provided some real confirmation for things
I'd long suspicioned but that didn't make sense! Or did They?

Things like pale faced me, with 50% Irish DNA, having at least part of my
DNA comprised of Native American, African, and European Jewish makeup.

I long suspicioned it, but until it was confirmed in My DNA
I hardly dared mention any of it, for fear of being ridiculed for such fantastic
thinking! Yet, there it is, proven through DNA.

Sometimes, I think our little Hunches, and sometimes our little Lunches,
all speak to us about where we originated.

Yes, I love to cook and bake, and perhaps someday I'll do a
Potato Story and Cook Book titled, "From Irish Roots"
based on my Irish Ancestry and Strong Irish Ethnicity.

What little intricacies, habits, food preferences, and other
unique aspects of your life come from Your Ancestry and DNA?

Of all the DNA Tests available, I believe Ancestry's Autosomal DNA Testing
does the best job of reaching back to antiquity while also providing great
Genealogical Connections.

# Cousin Matches

This is one area on which we could spend a lot of time.
It really only pertains to those who have had, or will have a DNA Test.

There was a time when having a DNA Test made me a little worried,
and I know there are some people who still feel that way.

There are also some people who believe they are sort of "hokey",
however based on what I've discovered, and learned along the way,
about our Family, it has led me to great DNA Cousin matches!

I had my Autosomal DNA Test done at Ancestry.ca,
three years ago, and it is still leading me to new discoveries.
It is quite simple to do, and now it has become quite affordable.

I really believe that everyone wanting to learn more about themselves,
their family, and their ethnicity, really can benefit from this Testing.

Besides, my DNA has been out there, for sometime.
and so far no one has done me any harm!

So, You might be wondering how having my DNA done has helped me?
Not only have I had some things confirmed as to where my origins are,
It's helped me make some breakthroughs!

Some of these breakthroughs come in the way of Cousin Matches
leading to, or narrowing down some of our family's most difficult mysteries.

One of these being the Ancestry of my Birth Mother.
You see, My Birth Mother was born out of Wedlock,
and her Mother had her before She was married.

Now, we all but have the answer as to who Her Father was!
This due to approximately 40 Cousin Matches!

# Ancestry DNA gives you more ...

Surprisingly, while I literally have Thousands of Cousin Matches,
they continue to come in.

The most surprising ones are those that have appeared over the past few
months. Forty, or so, that seem to indicate who my Birth Mother's Father was.

My birth Mother, Eleanor "Eileen" Marie (Burrill) Hurlburt, was born in 1930
Since that was less than 100 Years ago We are unable to get Her Birth Record.

However, we believe she was born in Halifax, Nova Scotia, Canada.
Where her family lived at that time.

Now, after Decades of research, based on DNA Cousin Matches,
I believe , regarding the identity of Her Father,
We can narrow it down to 4 likely Suspects!

All of these being Sons of John Richard Newcombe (1855-1924)
and Mary Catherine Edwards (1864-1952)

I now have nearly 40 Cousin Matches
who lead to the Newcombe Family of the Eastern Shore,
of Nova Scotia, in Halifax Regional Municipality.

The closest of these DNA Cousin Matches are
Descendant of John R. Newcombe and Mary C. Edwards.

So, while I may never know for certain, who my Grand Father was,
I am pretty confident that based on DNA, and Cousin Matches,
John R. Newcombe and Mary C. Edwards, are My Ancestors!

Thus, I now know at least part of My Mother's unknown Ancestry.
It was made possible through Ancestry's Autosomal DNA Testing
and the Resulting Cousin Matches!

# Ancestry Helps You Understand Your Genealogy.

"Ancestry" does require a Paid Membership,
following a 14 Day Free Trial Membership.
Yet, it has so much to offer, when it comes to understanding Your Genealogy.

I spent my first 20 years exhausting Free Resources, both online and off.

Getting my Ancestry Membership really helped propel my Research,
especially when combined with DNA Testing and Cousin Matches.
Ancestry is, in my opinion, one of the best resources online today!

When You create Your family tree, Hints appear!
The Hints take You to other Members Trees.

There You can view and compare what You have, with Their Findings.

This process can take you back many generations,
on what is reputed to be the world's largest collection of online records.

Again, remember, no matter where You are, online or otherwise,
the information you find is only as good as the Source.

Using another person's Tree on Ancestry, or elsewhere,
is a good way to find information,
but relying on their information, even if it's found in numerous Trees,
is not a good idea, unless it can be verified with actual Historical Records.

This is not always possible!

However, the thing to note here is that there are a number of people
who simply copy what they find, without ever taking time to look for, or
provide, a good Source for their findings. Then, sadly, their work is copied, over
and over again, by unsuspecting, well intentioned people.

**Don't become one of "Those People"!**

# Ancestry DNA Provides Detail and Historical Insights

Ancestry DNA provides precise geographic detail and clear-cut historical
insights, connecting you to the places where your story is truly rooted.


Truly helping provide everything from unique regions
to living relatives through DNA Cousin Matching.


Combining DNA results with the largest collection of records
to give the best insight into your genealogy, origins, and Cousin Matches.


Ancestry values privacy and uses industry standard security practices,
the latest cutting edge Autosomal testing technology, and advanced science,
combined with the world's largest online family history resource,
to predict genetic ethnicity and help find new family connections
through DNA Cousin Matches.


Ancestry DNA uses information from across 500 regions
identifying potential relatives through DNA matching
to others who have taken the Ancestry DNA test.


Your results are a great starting point
for more family history research, and it can also be a way to
dig even deeper into the research you've already done.


While Ancestry DNA may predict if you have Native American Ancestry,
from the U.S., Canada and Mexico,
the results do not currently provide a specific tribal affiliation,
and can not be used for legal documentation.


Once ordered, the Ancestry DNA kit arrives in the mail.
It includes full instructions, a saliva collection tube, and pre-paid return mailer.


After processing in the lab, You'll receive an email notifying you
your results are ready to explore on the Ancestry Website

# LIST OF RESOURCES

Resources can be found on our Website: growingyourfamilytree.com

Legacy Family Tree - The Database Software I use for My Genealogy

Google Search - Google provides great Search Results

"Yarmouth, Nova Scotia: A Sequel to Campbell's History"
Book by George S. Brown

The Izaak Walton Killam Memorial Library in Yarmouth, Nova Scotia

The Yarmouth County Museum and Archives in Yarmouth, Nova Scotia

Find A Grave - World's Largest Gravesite Collection

Automated Genealogy - Hosts Indexed Canadian Census Records

The Library and Archives Canada - Databases and other Research Tools

Nova Scotia Vital Stats - Searchable database containing one million names

Provincial Archives of New Brunswick - Vital Statistics Government Records

Prince Edward Island Public Archives and Records - Vital Statistics Records

Newfoundland Records - Collection of Records at FamilySearch

WikiTree: The Free Family Tree - Growing a single family tree database

Généalogie Acadienne - Acadian Research (Français & English Versions)

Ged Match - Provides DNA and genealogical analysis tools

MyHeriage - Online Family Tree, DNA Testing, Census, & Vital Stats Records

FamilyTreeDNA - DNA Testing for Ancestry & Genealogy

Ancestry  Website & DNA Testing

# Closing Thoughts

I hope You've enjoyed this Book,
and that you'll enjoy Your Research even more!

For me it began back in 1991, some 28 years ago!

It seems impossible that it's been that long,
it certainly has been a great journey!

I've always been a bit different, in a good way, I think!

My Father, Locke Hurlburt fathered me when he was 61 and
His Wife, Eleanor "Eileen" Marie Burrill was 25 years Younger,
a mere 36 years of age!

When I was all of 13 months
one of my Siblings cut my fingers off on my Right Hand!

I honestly tell people it's the best thing that ever happened to me!

The reason I say this is because
when I left Hospital after having my fingers put back on,
my Parents were wisely told I needed to be somewhere
away from the other children for a year to allow my fingers to heal.

As a result I went to live with Victor Hurlburt and His Wife, Enid (Outhouse)

After I was there for a month, Vic looked down at me,
and said, "If You call me Daddy I'll keep You"

Even though, at that point, I was a very shy and backward child,
I looked up and called Him, "Daddy"

Thus I was Adopted, and that afforded me Opportunities,
Opportunities My Siblings in My Birth Family did not have!

That's why I tell people that getting my fingers cut off
was the best thing that ever happened to me!

This all led to Me having Older Parents,
and many of their Friends became My Friends.
This led me to have a rather unique outlook on life.

Victor and Enid, my Mom & Dad,
provided me a great upbringing.
Not that we ever had a lot,
but we were never hungry.

Dad had been an "Acting CPO" at the end of WW II
which meant He trained the Men.

When I was in Grade 7, at about age 12,
My Friends took me aside and Told Me to Stop Marching!

I didn't even know that I was!

My Mom, Enid, was Your stereotypical Protestant Church Lady,
which gave me some interesting perspectives.

I tell You all this because it sort of sets the basis
for my research into Family History.

Having older Parents, both by Birth, and by Adoption,
gave me a unique outlook and
understanding of Life.

Leading me to Decades of Research
in many areas, especially
Genealogy, and Family History.

Which has become a wonderful pastime,
and will become my Life's Legacy.

I hope this Book will help You on Your Family History Journey.

May Your Research so Enrich Your Life, and the Lives of Others.

*Brian W. Hurlburt*